Original title:
Wristbands and Wavelengths

Author: Zachary Prescott
ISBN HARDBACK: 978-1-80586-051-8
ISBN PAPERBACK: 978-1-80586-523-0

Beat of the Belts

When I dance, I lose my pants,
The buckle's loose, it takes a chance.
My friends all laugh, I take a bow,
It’s a trendy style, who wore it how?

With a spin, my belly shows,
My clumsy moves steal all the shows.
They tie me down, I break away,
In the groove, we laugh and sway.

Frequency of Friendship

A tune we share, on loop we play,
It's worth the laughs, come what may.
The jokes we crack, a silly tune,
In silly hats, we dance by moon.

Our voices rise, a loud duet,
In harmony, there's no regret.
We sing off-key, but that's okay,
In friendship's band, we find our way.

Strands of Sound

In tangled thoughts, we twist and spin,
A loud guitar, absurdity's grin.
With every chord, our spirits soar,
We dance around like never before.

A jingle here, a giggle there,
Our laughter fills the open air.
Together we're a quirky crew,
In every strum, a funny view.

The Fabric of Togetherness

In stitches bright, we patch our seams,
With every joke, we fuel our dreams.
Our fabric woven, quirky threads,
With every laugh, we drop our dread.

A color clash, a riot of hues,
With every prank, we share our views.
Together we're a tapestry,
In our odd ways, we're fancy free.

Melodies of the Material

In a land where colors clash,
Bright bands tickle the wrist,
They jive with every splash,
Making shadows dance and twist.

Each one tells a silly tale,
Of a cat who learned to swim,
Or a dog who loves to scale,
The heights where light is dim.

When friends gather, the laughter swells,
Like bubbles in a fizzy drink,
With each snap, a story tells,
Of silly moments—what you think?

So wear your flashy, funky cheer,
And let the vibes connect with flair,
For in this jest, we all appear,
As dancing fools beyond compare.

Artifacts of Affinity

A rainbow wrapped around the arm,
Like a secret agent’s charm,
Each piece has its quirky grace,
You can’t help but smile and embrace.

One sparkles like a disco ball,
While others resemble sticky gum,
In the crowd, they call and brawl,
For the best spot at the drum.

A mishap leads to tangled fate,
As they unite in wobbly swing,
It's a fashion show, don’t be late,
Get your groove on, feel the zing!

With every laugh, connections grow,
In this silly bandit’s spree,
Wear them high, wear them low,
Together, we create the glee.

The Chorus of Connections

Under the sun, the colors gleam,
A circus parade on an urban street,
Each band sings its own wild theme,
In this quirky, rhythmic beat.

Tangled up like old shoelaces,
We dance to our eccentric tune,
Through all the funny faces,
Even raccoons join the monsoon!

A hop, a skip, then a flop,
We twirl and spin without a care,
As laughter rises to the top,
A heartbeat shared in the air.

In this chorus, we unite,
With mismatched styles and wild dreams,
Every chuckle feels just right,
As friendship binds our funny schemes.

Vibrations in the Air

In a world where colors sway,
Each hue dances in gay array.
Frogs wear hats, the cats just prance,
As silly jokes lead the chance.

A green giraffe jumps high and low,
While flamingos steal the show.
With every bounce, a giggle breaks,
And laughter rides on funky flakes.

Patterns of Unity

The socks have paired in strange delight,
Arguing who will take the flight.
Twists and turns, they form a chain,
As rabbits hop through rainbow rain.

Fried eggs are dancing on the floor,
While pancakes sing, 'We're wanting more!'
In bubbly bands, they sway and spin,
A breakfast disco, let’s begin!

Colorful Currents

Here comes a fish in neon shoes,
With zesty stripes, it just can't lose.
Butterflies flip, the clouds turn pink,
While squirrels play with vests that blink.

Jellybeans jump and twirl about,
Kites are laughing with a shout.
As fizzy drinks pop in delight,
The world is bright, both day and night.

Pulse of the Interwoven

Underneath a blanket of fluff,
The kittens argue, “Who’s more tough?”
They weave a tale of dangling dreams,
With giggles bouncing like silly streams.

A hedgehog roller-skates on grass,
While mice in tuxes cheer and clash.
Their silly whimsy fuels the cheer,
In this patchwork world, fun is near!

Sonic Strings of Memory

In a drawer I find, a colorful mess,
A rubbery festival, I must confess.
Each one holds a story, a laugh or a cheer,
A pop of nostalgia, the memories near.

I've got a green one that dances on air,
Every time I wave it, friends stop and stare.
A red one for shouting, a blue for a wink,
They giggle and jive, making hearts sync.

The Fabric of Interwoven Dreams

Tangled yarn of laughter, colors that gleam,
A patchwork of moments, each stitch a dream.
With threads of delight, we sew up the fun,
A fabric of friendship, a race to be won.

When I pull on the yellow, the giggles all rise,
The purple one whispers, a truth in disguise.
A tapestry bright, memory's dance,
In knots of joy, we twirl and prance.

Harmony in the Hands

In colorful circles, my thoughts take flight,
A mix of the silly and pure delight.
Each twist and each turn, a laugh we can share,
With fingers entwined, we float in the air.

The orange one hums, a tune from the past,
While the pink one is quick, spreading joy at last.
In concert we giggle, a symphony bright,
Creating our rhythm, from morning to night.

Links of Sound and Sentiment

Bright loops of laughter, a chain of our love,
Each bounce and each jig, like a dance from above.
The jingles and jangles, they echo our cheer,
Connected together, we hold memories dear.

A clink and a clatter, a melody sweet,
With each little hop, we sway to the beat.
Links of sheer joy, as we joke and we play,
In colors of friendship, forever we stay.

Colors in Concert

In a world where colors play,
They groove and swirl in bright dismay.
A red twirls with a funky beat,
While blue pulls off some fancy feet.

Green does the cha-cha with a twist,
Orange claims it's the color of bliss.
Yellows pop with a cheerful shout,
While purples just dance about.

Their shades collide in playful cheer,
Finding harmony when they appear.
A rainbow riot, laughter prevails,
In this colorful union, joy never fails.

Energy Enmeshed

Zingy vibes float in the air,
Bouncing round without a care.
Charged ideas mix and blend,
Each giggle a twist, a twist to send.

Buzzy dances light up the night,
Sparks of fun in every sight.
A jolt of laughter, a playful zap,
Life’s a circuit, we’re all in the lap.

Energy flows in silly beats,
With every twirl, the joy completes.
Watt's the fun? It's electric cheer,
When we blend the vibes, the party’s here!

Emotions in Motion

A giggle spins, a tear takes flight,
Laughter bounces, pure delight.
Joy jumps high, sadness drifts down,
Together they twirl, a quirky crown.

Anger stomps with a heavy shoe,
While calm sways gently, feeling new.
Every feeling finds its dance,
In this quirky song, who knows the chance?

Wobbly moods do the funky sway,
Chasing blues far, far away.
In this motion, we all feel free,
In funny forms, we skip with glee.

Mutual Frequencies

Tickle the air, a sound collides,
Bouncing waves, where fun abides.
Frequency flows, a playful slap,
Resonance making us all clap.

A melody bursts, laughter's embrace,
Echoing joy all over the place.
In sync with giggles that rise and fall,
Finding rhythm, a tune for us all.

Chords of friendship, silly and bright,
Humming together in pure delight.
These mighty waves, they twist and glide,
Together we laugh, never to hide.

Vibrant Chains

On my wrist, a rainbow glows,
Each bead a tale that tickles the nose.
Friends often ask, "What's the fuss?"
I just smile, it’s all in the dust!

Straps of colors, twists and bends,
A silly charm that never ends.
Together they dance, oh what a sight,
In the morning sun, they feel just right.

Shimmering Symbols

A glimmering charm rides the wave,
It's a fashion statement, oh so brave!
Friends say, "Wow, what a bling!"
I reply, "It's my circus ring!"

With every clip and jingle sound,
Laughter echoes all around.
It's more than style, it's pure delight,
Dressed to impress, shining so bright.

Threads of Time

My wrist a tapestry, vibrant and bold,
Each thread a memory lovingly told.
"You wear the past?" my pals might tease,
I say, "Yes, and I'm feeling at ease!"

From parties to picnics, each one a hit,
My knotted treasures are quite the fit.
Tickles and giggles, I wear with pride,
In life's grand parade, I take each stride.

Notes in the Knots

A jingle here, a jangle there,
My arm's a band, with style to spare.
Each little knot, a giggle contained,
In this wild symphony, I'm unchained!

As friends join in, the laughter climbs,
While we twist and tangle in playful rhymes.
Note by note, we weave in fun,
In our concert of chaos, we’re never done!

Bands of Connection

In a world where colors blend,
Some patterns make us laugh, my friend.
The ties that wrap around our wrists,
A hidden code in playful twists.

They jingle when we dance and sway,
A mark of friendship on display.
Worn proudly like a badge of cheer,
These tokens whisper, 'I am here!'

Like rubber bands they stretch and bend,
Creating bonds that never end.
In quirky styles, we all partake,
Stitched memories we love to make.

Echoes in the Fiber

In the threads of laughter, we weave,
A tapestry that won't deceive.
Colors clash in joyous jives,
Each one tells how our spirit thrives.

With wacky styles, we strut about,
Making faces that scream and shout.
These fibers hold a silent tune,
Dancing hearts beneath the moon.

Each twist and turn brings giggles near,
In a spectrum loud and clear.
A fashion statement so bizarre,
Like picking up a yellow car!

Spectrum of Sentiments

In hues of laughter, bright and bold,
We crochet stories yet untold.
Each shade reflects a silly time,
Unruly verses without a rhyme.

A rainbow flows from hand to hand,
Unique connections we all planned.
Their wobbly forms, a playful freak,
In every twist, our joy can speak.

With quirky shapes both far and wide,
We hug each meme and silly stride.
A fashion show of jest and quirk,
In every color, friendship lurks.

Ties That Bind

With stretchy cords and goofy flair,
These ties reveal our bond so rare.
We twiddle and twist, we pull along,
Creating laughs and silly songs.

From red to blue, a playful race,
We wrap each other's quirks with grace.
In every chuckle, there's a hug,
Like finding a warm, fuzzy bug.

When mischief calls, we'll jump and cheer,
The world awaits with grins so dear.
With funky cords, we spin and glide,
In laughter's arm, we'll always bide.

Chords of Companionship

In a world where colors clash,
And stripes dance with a flash,
We laugh at styles so absurd,
Matching hues without a word.

Our arms entwined like silly vines,
A duet played with clumsy lines,
Each jingle tells a playful tale,
In harmony, we'll never fail.

When one of us decides to twirl,
The others join in with a whirl,
Oh, the styles we all embrace,
Laughing together, we own the space.

So here's to ties that make us grin,
With every laugh, we surely win,
In this colorful, clumsy spree,
Together, we create glee.

Binds of Belief

In goofy colors, we trust our fate,
Snapping bands like a playful gait,
Each stretch a promise, a silly pact,
In this silly game, there's no act.

Let's mock the serious with our flair,
Wacky designs that make people stare,
For every laugh, a knot tied tight,
In this funky fabric, we find our light.

We challenge norms with every twist,
In this eccentric circle, who can resist?
A fabric bond, so bright and bold,
A comedic chapter, waiting to unfold.

So wear your colors, loud and proud,
In the chaos, we're a happy crowd,
With every snap, our spirits rise,
In this funny dance, we are the prize.

Tuning into Threads

We strut around in mismatched glee,
A cacophony of threads, can’t you see?
Each loop and twist a tune to hum,
In this wild tapestry, we’re all so fun.

With every color, a joke unwinds,
A symphony of laughter, joy it finds,
In silly patterns, we sway and twirl,
United by threads, we just want to whirl.

Our fashion sense, a sight to see,
With quirky knots, we’re wild and free,
Each laugh a note in this joyous song,
In the rhythm of us, we all belong.

So let’s celebrate our tangled vibe,
In this riot of style, let’s not hide,
Together we sing, forever we thread,
With laughter and color, we forge ahead.

Chasing Currents

With every twist, we chase the breeze,
Silly patterns that aim to please,
Like waves of laughter rippling around,
In this joyful current, we are found.

Strange designs glide in the air,
Matching chaos, without a care,
Our colors clash in a playful spree,
In this funny flow, we're wild and free.

Each band a tale, each thread a laugh,
Navigating life's whimsical path,
With goofy grins and carefree ways,
In the pulse of joy, we spend our days.

So ride the waves of silly dreams,
In a whirl of colors, nothing's as it seems,
Together we'll dance in vibrant streams,
Chasing the currents, living our dreams.

Echoes of Color and Connection

In neon hues that twist and twirl,
A fashion statement with a whirl.
Each flicker shines, it's quite a sight,
As friends declare, "This looks just right!"

The echo laughs as colors clash,
Like rainbows diving in a splash.
We wear our pride without a care,
In quirky styles, we take the dare!

From polka dots to stripes so wide,
A circus act we can't abide.
With mismatched tones and playful flair,
We strut around, a vibrant pair!

So come and join this merry crew,
Where color bursts in every hue.
With giggles shared and hearts aligned,
In this wild world, our joy you'll find!

Threads of Vibration

A thread pulls tight, we smile and sway,
Each tiny jiggle makes our day.
When fabric dances, all is well,
With tales of laughter, oh can you tell?

In tangled knots, our stories weave,
A whirling dervish, make-believe!
With one loud pop, the colors blend,
A silly saga without end.

Like rubber ducks that float in line,
Our threads unite, the stars align.
They stretch and bounce, a joyful play,
In hidden seams, our dreams will stay!

So grab a friend, it’s time to twist,
In this chaotic fashion mist.
With every giggle and crazy spin,
We're sewn together, let’s begin!

The Pulse of Fabric and Sound

A thumping heart in every stitch,
As music weaves through every glitch.
The beat drops low, we leap in time,
With fabric moves, oh so sublime!

Who knew a shirt could dance so bold?
With patterns etched in stories told.
As laughter fills the air so sweet,
The rhythm makes us move our feet!

As jackets shimmy in the breeze,
They serenade the buzzing trees.
With every twirl, a vibrant sound,
In our tapestry of joy, we're found!

So let’s embrace this fabric thrill,
With friends we find the joyful spill.
In every tug and playful slide,
Together we will take the ride!

Spectrum of Silence

In hush of hues, a cheeky grin,
A silent dance about to begin.
With colors bright and shades of cheek,
We giggle loud, though words are weak.

Our outfits speak in whispers grand,
While silence rules our laughter band.
With every shade that draws a wink,
We wave and swirl 'til hearts all sink!

Invisible ties, we bounce about,
In quiet chaos, dance and shout.
The spectrum swirls, a playful sight,
In colors mute, we find our light!

So join the fun, let laughter rise,
In silent waves under the skies.
With every blink, our joy will show,
A vivid dream in silence flow!

Signals in the Silhouette

A readout on my arm, oh what a sight,
The colors swirl like a disco light.
I wave to you, you mimic my flair,
Our pulses match, it's a tricky affair.

A chat with my wrist, it's all the rage,
It speaks in tones, a digital sage.
When it glitches, I dance like a fool,
Trying to fix it, it's really uncool.

We laugh as it buzzes, oh what a tease,
It's not a pet, but it sure has its whims.
With every tick, there's a jolly message,
Unintended comedy in a tech-based visage.

So here's to signals, and silly times,
In-sync we move with our jester rhymes.
Our shadows mingle in a silly light,
As we march to the beat, of laughter tonight.

Tapestry of Touch

With threads of color, I sew my fate,
Each tug a giggle, each pull a rate.
They say wear this, it’s trendy and fine,
But I think I’m actually a walking design.

When you poke at mine, it blinks and shines,
A conversation starter, we draw the lines.
You tug on my sleeve, and I spin around,
A fashion statement, in laughter I'm bound.

The patterns we wear tell stories, it’s true,
But who knew that blue could feel like a zoo?
With every caress, I’ll break into song,
A tapestry woven, where we all belong.

So here’s to the moments, funny and bright,
Each strand a connection, a delightful sight.
In this quirky corner, we spin and we twirl,
Creating a dance in this colorful whirl.

Harmonies of Hope

In a world where signals chat and greet,
My arm is a stage, where rhythms meet.
With each little buzz, I spark a jest,
From awkward dance moves, I’m truly blessed.

Chatting away with the flick of a wrist,
Echoes of laughter in every twist.
A song of the silly, a chorus of joy,
Regardless of issues, I’ll still be your toy.

The harmonies beckon, we laugh till we cry,
Errors not failures, they just fly by.
With every misstep, we're creating a show,
Imperfect perfection, that’s how we grow.

So let’s raise a toast to the sounds that we create,
Our own little band, let’s celebrate fate.
In a world full of antics, we’ll dance through the strife,
In rhythms of camaraderie, we’ll celebrate life.

Threads of Light

A flicker, a flash, our signal is clear,
With threads of bright colors, I rise from the drear.
The glow on my wrist, a beacon of fun,
Every laugh we share, we've only begun.

We prance like peacocks, adorned and bold,
These threads weave tales that never get old.
When connections fizzle, we just have a blast,
Making memories, oh, how they last!

Like shooting stars in a midnight spree,
These bright little lights echo our glee.
Interwoven giggles beam through the night,
As we dance and twirl, everything feels right.

So here's to the glow and the crazy delight,
With threads of connection that shine so bright.
In the tapestry of laughter, we find our way,
With every silly moment, let's play and sway!

Radiance of Relations

In a rainbow of colors we trust,
Each friend flashes bright, like a must.
We trade silly stories, a giggle fest,
Knotted together, we laugh with the best.

Like a parade of quirks on our arms,
Each charm, a tale, holds its own charms.
From bright polka dots to stripes so grand,
Together we'll dance, hand in hand.

When one pulls a prank, the other's on cue,
Like magnets of mischief, we stick like glue.
With wearable joys, we strut and we sway,
Turning every dull moment into play.

So here's to the laughter that stitches our days,
The colorful madness, the silly displays.
In this wacky collection, I've found my tribe,
United in laughter, we come alive!

Fields of Fabric

In fields of fabric, we frolic about,
Each piece a wrinkle, a giggle, no doubt.
Wrap me up tightly in threads of pure glee,
We'll splice silly tales, just you and me.

With patterns so wild, we'll steal every show,
From sequins to stripes, oh the places we'll go!
Spinning around in a whirl of delight,
We'll twirl like confetti, oh what a sight!

Laughter embroidered in each quirky fold,
Decorating friendships like treasures untold.
With threads that are tangled, we're always a pair,
In this vibrant circus, there's magic to share.

So grab your colors, let's weave the fun,
In this fabric of life, we've already won!
With patterns of humor, we'll dance through the day,
In our fields of fabric, let's play, play, play!

Resonant Reflections

Bouncing laughter like sounds in the air,
We echo our quirks, and none can compare.
Mirrored in chaos, we find our own beat,
Reflecting such joy, it's quite the treat!

With every loud giggle, a ripple is made,
Our jokes are like waves, they never fade.
In this pond of fun, we splash all around,
Creating a chorus of silly sound.

So put on your shades, shine bright like the sun,
With friends by your side, it's a guaranteed fun!
From silly reflections to jokes that won't stop,
In this world of laughter, we'll always swap!

Every twist and turn, each fun little jibe,
Is captured in moments that we all describe.
United in humor, our bond's quite strong,
In this resonant symphony, we all belong!

Fabricated Bonds

From threadbare giggles to stitches of cheer,
We craft our connections, that's perfectly clear.
With patches of laughter, we sew up the day,
Creating a quilt that is vibrant and gay.

Each knot that we tie adds a tale to our tale,
Creating new memories that never grow pale.
From fabric of jest, we weave our delight,
With each quirky twist, we'll take to the night.

As we parade through the streets, what a sight,
With our ensemble of fun, everything feels right.
From one-liners to pranks, we craft our own song,
In this fabric of life, we'll always belong!

So here's to the threads that connect us all,
In this patchwork of laughter, we'll never fall.
With fabricated bonds, our joy will persist,
In a world full of color, we simply can't miss!

Shapes of Synergy

In a world of colors, bright and bold,
We twist and turn, never doing what we're told.
Crafted loops and ties, so neat,
A party on our wrists, oh, what a treat!

Laughing at the way they glide,
Like a dance of joy, side by side.
Each shape a story, silly and grand,
Tangled tales, oh isn't it planned?

Who knew these threads could connect us all,
In a jumbled mess, we stand tall.
With colors clashing, a vibrant sight,
Cackles erupt with sheer delight!

Watch them shimmer, watch them sway,
As we celebrate this quirky display.
With every twist, we cheer and grin,
In this rhythm of laughter, we all win!

The Language of Looms

Words can be tricky, but colors so fun,
In the world of threads, we all come undone.
We weave our stories, honest and sly,
Speaking in patterns that catch the eye.

Each loop a message, crammed with cheer,
What did I say? Oh dear, let's be clear!
A knot in the language, a twist to please,
We giggle and fumble - oh, as we tease!

New styles emerge, ever so bright,
A palette of nonsense, all day and night.
From crazy designs to patterns that clash,
What a sight we create in an artistic flash!

So grab your loom, let's start a spree,
Crafting our tales, wild as can be.
In each little thread, let laughter bloom,
In this fabric of friendship, let's create room!

Pulse and Pattern

With vibrant beats, our spirits rise,
Each twist a rhythm, a sweet surprise.
Patterns that dance on our happy arms,
Spreading laughter with all their charms.

Wiggling and jiggling, a colorful mess,
A symphony swirls in our playful dress.
Oh look! A twist that's lost its way,
Let's chase that loop, come what may!

Funky and fresh, we pulse in sync,
Laughing at colors that make us think.
In each little surge, we find our groove,
Wiggly wonders that make us move!

So grab your mates, let's make some noise,
In our crazy styles, we discover joys.
Echoing laughter, a bright parade,
Life in full color, never displayed!

Unseen Attachments

Tangled in threads, we form a bond,
Invisible ties, of which we're fond.
A curious jumble, no need to see,
Just trust the joy in our lunacy!

With goofy grins, we tie a bow,
Every knot a secret, merrily on show.
The more we twist, the more we connect,
Laughter is our glue, oh what a effect!

Strange little charms that dangle and sway,
In unseen links, we find our way.
Oh the giggles when one goes astray,
Catching silly moments, come what may!

So here’s to the bonds that make us cheer,
In the art of the absurd, we hold dear.
With every twist, let the fun unfold,
In our tangled tales, let laughter be told!

Interlaced Frequencies

In a world full of chatter, they dance and they sway,
Bouncing to rhythms, in a light-hearted way.
Colors collide, a spectrum so bright,
The laughter around them, a charming delight.

Snug on the wrist, like a friendship so true,
Joking and jiving, they wiggle anew.
Each twist and each turn, a giggle in tune,
They sing in the sun, under the chuckling moon.

Bound with a promise, they stretch and they play,
Telling old stories in their quirky display.
A tap here, a flick there, they shimmy with flair,
Who knew such fibers could make us all care?

When the band goes quiet, you won't see them frown,
They simply recharge, ready to clown.
For each little twist, a joke left to weave,
Endless the giggles—who could ever believe?

The Symphony of Straps

Once upon a band that loved to perform,
Comedic chaos was their typical norm.
They played silly symphonies, loud and absurd,
While wearing their stripes, they laughed and they stirred.

With a jingle and jangle, they caused quite a scene,
Whenever they wiggled, it was pure caffeine.
Each strap made a sound like a rubbery squeak,
Syncing their madness with a rhythm unique.

Onlookers chuckled at their carefree jest,
“Why wear fancy gems when this is the best?”
With a flick and a flutter, the crowd could not breathe,
For the symphony’s magic—who'd want to leave?

The echoes of laughter would linger and play,
As bands made the music to dance night away.
So join the parade, wear a strap full of cheer,
And let the world grin when you bring up the rear.

Links of Emotion

Tangled together, a chain of delight,
With giggles and grins, they light up the night.
Each link tells a story, each twist is a joke,
Laughter that flows like shimmering smoke.

They wiggle in unison, sharing their quirks,
An army of joy—where everyone smirks.
In gatherings loud, or in whispers so small,
They unite in a bond that could charm one and all.

Bouncing like rubber, like springs on a spree,
They wear their emotions, wild and so free.
A tap on the wrist, oh, what a grand show,
A humorous dance, and the vibes overflow!

As night drifts away on the wings of a dream,
The links hold their secret—a funny team beam.
Together through chaos, they flutter and blend,
For the laughter continues, and it will never end!

Radiant Ribbons

In a swirl of colors, let the ribbons collide,
Wrapped up in laughter, they flourish with pride.
Carefree confetti, they tumble and twist,
Creating a spectacle, who could resist?

Look at them giggle, those looped and whirled bands,
They frolic and bounce like wild little hands.
Unruly and fun, in the sunlight they gleam,
Launching a magic that's bursting at the seams.

With playful encounters, they stretch and they sway,
Dancing through moments in their own silly way.
When caught in a breeze, they flutter and drift,
Like rain on a sunny day, they're quite the gift!

In hues of hilarity, they charm and they tease,
A whimsical fiesta, blowing away the unease.
So grab a few ribbons, let laughter ignite,
For the magic of humor makes everything right!

Waves of Unity and Belief

In the ocean of jests, we float so high,
Making ripples and splashes, oh my, oh my!
With a wink and a giggle, we ride the tide,
A boatload of laughter where good times abide.

Bouncing along like a fish on a spree,
Casting lines of humor, just you and me.
We surf on the memes of a digital sea,
With every wave crashing, we're wild and free.

Chords Woven in Time

Strumming on strings like a cat with flair,
Dancing in circles with socks to spare.
With each pluck of joy, the notes intertwine,
Creating a symphony that's purely divine.

Like noodles in soup, we twist and we turn,
As melodies of laughter cause songs to churn.
We're a band of misfits, harmonizing bright,
In the concert of chaos, we take flight.

Echoing Ties of Emotion

In the laughter of echoes, we find our place,
Jumping through memories like a playful race.
With the sound of our chuckles, we bridge the gap,
Strings of connection in a silly mishap.

Shouting to the void, we hear it reply,
With a burst of delight, we reach for the sky.
Every giggle a ripple, each pun a flare,
In this cosmic joke, we're floating in air.

Frequencies of Friendship

In the wireless world, we tune up our laughs,
Counting the moments, like math with some halves.
Every signal and giggle sends waves through the air,
Frequenting joy in a friendship so rare.

Dancing to vibes that are quirky and fun,
Synchronized humor, we're never outdone.
With a beat that's contagious and jokes that ignite,
In the playlist of life, we shine so bright.

Fabric of our Frequencies

In a world where colors clash,
We giggle at the patterns rash.
Stripes and polka dots collide,
Friendship's fabric, side by side.

A tapestry of joy we weave,
With every stitch, we can't believe.
Each loop a laugh, each knot a cheer,
Our scrapbook lives, so bright and clear.

When one goes missing, oh what a fright,
Then back they come, no need to fight.
A jumbled mess of joyful threads,
We wear our quirks like cozy spreads.

So here's to us, the quirky crew,
With mismatched threads, and colors too.
In every hug, a bond that sings,
Wrapped in humor, life’s silly things.

The Pulse of Togetherness

Beats collide in happy waves,
We dance like dolphins, all misbehaves.
The rhythm of friendship's a jolly spree,
With silly tunes just you and me.

A heartbeat shared on silly nights,
In cozy socks and shared delights.
When one falls down, we all just laugh,
Playing our silly, joyous half.

With every giggle, the pulse goes strong,
Our quirky beat, where we belong.
A symphony of jests and glee,
Together, we rock, just you and me!

So if you hear a silly sound,
Just know it’s joy spinning round.
In our goofy game, we twirl and sway,
Together forever, come what may.

Threads of Resonance

We're stitched together, a patchwork crew,
Sharing snacks and jokes, it's true.
With every chuckle, a thread we spin,
In our colorful world, we always win.

Each twirl and twist makes laughter soar,
Tangled together, oh, what a score!
A mix of colors, a joyful sight,
Our friendship shines, a vivid light.

When frazzled and frayed, we just unwind,
With every joke, a way to find.
The fabric of fun that keeps us tight,
In our quirky world, everything's right.

So here's to the madness, the joy we share,
The silly threads that show we care.
In this wacky quilt of life we face,
We're a comfy, laughing, happy place.

Frequencies of Fabric

In a jumbled world of colorful threads,
We giggle and weave on our merry beds.
With every punchline, we crank the dial,
Creating a frequency that makes us smile.

A colorful song in a fabric sea,
Our wacky rhythms are wild and free.
When one hits mute, we bring the cheer,
In our funny tunes, we disappear.

A kaleidoscope of humor bright,
Where every joke is pure delight.
We blend our quirks in harmony,
Dancing to the beat of shared glee.

So clap your hands and weave your song,
In our crazy world, we all belong.
With laughter echoing every day,
In this funny fabric, we'll always play.

Vibrating with Shared Moments

In a cozy café, we share a brew,
With laughs so loud, folks steal a view.
The clinks of cups, a funny tune,
As we dance to the rhythm of the afternoon.

A buzzing phone, a message so sly,
Did you mean to text, or just fly by?
Our giggles echo, without a care,
Like squirrels on caffeine, we're quite a pair.

A random photo, goofy faces made,
The world in slow-mo, our plans displayed.
With silly hats and winter socks,
We capture life in quirky blocks.

Connected through Resonance

Two friends chatting, the puns unfold,
In a world of humor, we break the mold.
A wink, a nudge, the fun ignites,
As we stir the pot of laughter bites.

“Did you just trip?” a jest in the air,
We laugh so hard, it’s quite a scare.
In synchrony, we tell our tales,
With playful jabs and goofy gales.

The echoes ripple, a comedic wave,
Every moment shared, the memories save.
Fearless in jest, we dance and sway,
Like wind-up toys lost in the fray.

Threads of Experience

A tangled yarn of stories spun,
Each twist and turn, revealing fun.
With colors bright, our lives entwined,
In this fabric of laughter, perfectly aligned.

Beneath the stars, we weave our fate,
With witty banter, we laugh till late.
Our hearts a tapestry, vibrant and bold,
Stitched with giggles and tales retold.

“Remember that time?” with grins we share,
The slip-ups and antics, we’ve laid it bare.
Each stitch a moment, each knot a smile,
In this quirky quilt, we stay awhile.

Synchronized Melodies

A melodic tune, we hum in sync,
Our voices shake, but we don’t blink.
With laughter leading, and puns in play,
We compose a symphony for the day.

Clumsy moves, while dancing too fast,
We trip over rhythms, but have a blast.
With every blunder, our spirits soar,
In this offbeat music, we want more.

The chorus builds, a humorous sound,
Within this concert, joy is found.
As we jam along, with hearts content,
In perfect disarray, our laughter's spent.

The Colorful Cadence of Life

In a world where shades collide,
A pink sock meets a blue tie wide.
They dance about with silly grace,
Strutting their stuff in a wild embrace.

Polka dots prance in the sun,
Singing songs that are just plain fun.
Butterflies giggle in the breeze,
As they tease the flowers with such ease.

A rainbow feast on a plate,
Carrots and jellybeans, what a fate!
They challenge your taste buds to a fight,
Bringing joy with every bite.

So gather your colors, your silly hats,
Join this circus of playful chats.
With laughter echoing in the air,
Life's vibrant colors become our dare.

Tethered by Tone

A chicken crossed a vibrant road,
Wearing headphones like it's a code.
It walked to the beat of a disco song,
Dancing all day, it couldn't be wrong.

The cows sway gently to the sound,
As the farmer's tunes whirl around.
They moo in harmony, not a care,
Creating a symphony rare and fair.

A cat with a bow tie struts with pride,
Meowing melodies as it glides.
Each purr a note on a bright scale,
Turning the garden into a funny tale.

So come join in this jolly spree,
With clothes that clash and spirits free.
In a rhythm that makes us twirl and spin,
Together we thrive, let the laughter in!

Knots of Understanding

Two friends gathered by the old oak,
Debating the best flavors of cake.
One swore by chocolate, the other by fruit,
Their laughter tangled, a silly pursuit.

With hands in knots over stories told,
They stumbled through memories, brave and bold.
Each tale a twist, a laugh, a tear,
Binding them closer with every cheer.

The sun played tricks through leaves above,
Casting shadows in a dance of love.
As giggles echoed through the air,
The knots of friendship were laid bare.

In the end, they feasted side by side,
On a mash-up of cake that couldn't hide.
For in every slice of laughter and cheer,
They found a connection that drew them near.

Rhythm of Connection

In a quirky town where misfits thrive,
A clock ticks backward, alive and jive.
The baker croons while mixing the dough,
Creating treats that steal the show.

The postman slides down a rainbow slide,
Delivering love with whimsical pride.
Each letter a melody wrapped in a hug,
Sparking smiles with every snug.

Cats in top hats strum the guitar,
While dogs breakdance under the stars.
The rhythm of lives all intertwined,
In this bizarre harmony, we all find.

So dance through life with a goofy grin,
As we syncopate joy from within.
For laughter is the beat, love is the song,
In this vibrant waltz, where we all belong.

Unbroken Threads

In the closet, mismatched pairs,
Dancing like they don't have cares.
Each color screaming, 'Pick me now!'
With fabric stories of 'Look at how!'

The cat thinks they're a tasty snack,
Chasing them down, no looking back.
They twirl and twist, so out of line,
Making me laugh, my heart's on shine.

Friends come over, we share a smile,
Wrapped in laughs, let's stay a while.
With threads like these, it's hard to frown,
In this fabric world, we wear the crown!

So here's to colors, bright and loud,
We weave our joy, we're so damn proud.
Giggles abound, we stitch the night,
In these silly threads, everything's right.

Fabrics of Fate

Woven tales and silly scenes,
Pillow fights and jelly beans.
What's on your shirt? Oh, what a sight!
A map of jelly, it feels just right.

Each fabric's got a tale to tell,
Like shouting socks saying 'Ring the bell!'
They throw a party in the drawer,
"I'm the loudest!" yells the floor.

A tie-dye dream stitched with glee,
Can make you laugh, just wait and see.
Wrap me up in threads of fun,
We share this joy till the day is done!

Stitching moments, oh so bright,
In this fabric dance, we take flight.
Together we laugh, this game of fate,
Unraveling stories from our crate!

Harmonizing Hues

Pick a color, what’s your mood?
Bright like sunshine, or maybe crude?
Twisting laughter like spun-up yarn,
In this spectrum, we all do charm.

A flick of green, a pop of red,
A rainbow party, let’s go ahead!
With every shade, our joy ignites,
Dancing in circles, scaling heights.

Checkered shoes and polka dots,
Create our groove, forget the thoughts.
Let’s spin and hop, a colorful race,
In our fancy threads, we’ll find our place!

When mismatched hues collide and twist,
You can’t resist this joyful tryst.
We laugh and twirl, our spirits swell,
In this fabric world, all’s well!

The Interlaced Journey

Off we go with hands so free,
Tangled up in jester glee.
Every loop and twist we make,
Brings hearty laughs, oh what a break!

A sock brigade, in search of fun,
Chasing shadows, on the run.
With threads connecting us in cheer,
We march together, skip a gear!

Through every snag and playful knot,
We stitch the smiles, forget what's hot.
With patterns bright, we pause and cheer,
What a journey, with friends so near!

So let’s interlace our tales tonight,
With silly antics, pure delight.
In this fabric of life, we find our place,
Laughing together, every embrace!

Cascading Colors

In a world of shades and hues,
My arm's a rainbow, making news.
With every flick and every twist,
I summon smiles, I can’t resist.

Bright pinks and yellows, quite the show,
Each combo causes quite a glow.
People ask, 'What’s your secret style?'
I wink and say, 'It’s all a while!'

A clash of dots, a flurry of stripes,
Fashion disasters? Not this type!
My wrist’s alive with colors bright,
Dancing shadows in the light.

When friends ogle at my dazzling flair,
I chuckle, 'It’s my fancy wear!'
From silly sparkles to neon grins,
I wear my art, where fun begins.

Mirrored Messages

On my wrist, a secret code,
Reflecting tales of every road.
A message caught in sparkly beads,
I smile, 'It's just some fun little deeds!'

Bouncing words from left to right,
'Laugh more!' they say, 'Just take flight!'
In laughs where every syllable gleams,
My wrist tells jokes, or so it seems.

Each bead's a laugh, each charm a pun,
A wristy wordsmith having fun.
They read the humor, loud and clear,
What joy it is to spread good cheer!

So come on by, get in the groove,
Let's construct a message with a move.
In this whirl of glimmer and light,
My wrist channels giggles, day and night.

The Poetry of Patterns

Lines and curves swirl ‘round my arm,
Each twist and turn, quite the charm.
Patterns singing, making me glee,
Whirlwinds of humor, just wait and see.

From stripes so bold to polka dots,
Cotton candy dreams, and silly thoughts.
I tap my wrist, a song begins,
Where laughter grows and fun never thins.

Spots of teal and pops of pink,
They giggle, wink, and make you think.
A scribble here, a squiggle there,
Can you guess what’s hiding, do you dare?

So unravel the art, come take a peek,
In every turn, there’s joy to seek.
With a giggle and a spin, you’ll see,
This patterned realm is wild and free.

Energies Entwined

A tangle here, a twist over there,
My wrist is buzzing, fun to share.
Colors clash in an energetic dance,
Who knew chaos could hold a chance?

Little charms like jolly sprites,
Jump and jive, oh what delights!
I sport this medley with a grin,
Where laughter bounces, love begins.

The mix and match, a playful spree,
Unruly beads, oh can't you see?
Each jingle adds to my joyful scheme,
Buzzing together, it's all a dream.

So join this whirlwind, let's commence,
A party on my wrist, in pure suspense.
With colors tangling and laughter so loud,
This joyous spectrum, let's share with the crowd.

Resonance in a Tangle

In a jumble of colors, who knows what's what?
A knot on my wrist, looks like a cat!
Each twist is a story, each loop is a joke,
I laugh at the mess, it's the ultimate poke.

Straps on my arm, they dance and they sway,
Like tiny performers, in a slapstick play.
They tickle my funny bone, a sight to behold,
In the circus of life, their antics unfold.

Elastic and quirky, they stretch and they bend,
Who knew a small trinket could transcend?
With all of their colors, they cheer and they peek,
In this funny parade, they seem quite unique.

Yet when I try to untangle this mess,
It's a puzzle so tricky, I must confess!
I tug and I pull, but they just laugh and cling,
My wrist is now royalty, adorned in a bling!

Bands of Harmony and Thought

These loops on my wrist, they're quite out of control,
Singing sweet tunes, like a quirky soul.
They argue in colors, a cacophony bright,
Each one has a mood, like day turns to night.

A red one is grumpy, a blue feels so chill,
The green is for giggles, the yellow a thrill.
Together they chatter, a melodic brigade,
In the orchestra of life, they perfectly wade.

Onlookers are baffled, they stare and they grin,
At this odd little band, where chaos begins.
But they can't hear the laughter, the joy that they bring,
Oh, how I adore this silly wrist bling!

If only my thoughts could be tangled so neat,
As these bands on my wrist keep dancing to beat.
Life's rhythm is funny, it twists and it turns,
With every new color, a lesson I learn!

Ties that Sing to the Heart

These loops tie me down, but I love how they sing,
Each note is a giggle, a fun little fling.
They bumble and bounce, in tactical play,
As my wrist prepares for a very wild day.

One's a proud prankster, another a tease,
Together they plot, with mischievous ease.
Each time they get tangled, a chuckle erupts,
Like a comedy show, where laughter interrupts.

Their melodies swirl like a whimsical breeze,
As they jingle and jangle, oh, how they please!
With every soft tug, a tune starts to grow,
In the orchestra's chaos, my giggles overflow.

So here's to the ties that bring joy to my day,
In shimmering colors, they waddle and sway.
With humor so bright, my heart they enchant,
Like a lively ensemble, to which I will rant!

The Fabric of Frequency

In a colorful frenzy, they twist and they twine,
These little creations, so silly, divine.
A rainbow of giggles, they vibrate in joy,
Each pulse is a laugh, like a child's favorite toy.

They stretch to the limits, then snap right back tight,
In this fabric of nonsense, everything feels right.
Every color's a frequency, each pattern a sound,
Dancing on my wrist, they spin round and round.

Jokes jive and jingle, in luminescent hues,
Who knew that their antics could promise such blues?
But they lighten the load, with their whimsical spin,
In a world full of chaos, they make me grin!

So here's to the fabric where fun never ends,
With every wild twist, my spirit ascends.
Forget all the worry, just laugh and unwind,
In this tapestry playful, pure joy you'll find!

Energy Embodied

In a world of tangled threads,
My wrist is quite the fashion dread.
Each color sparkles, jabs, and pokes,
Summoning giggles, not just jokes.

Rubber circles grip my wrist,
Each one claims a secret twist.
They bounce like kittens, full of cheer,
With every wave, they disappear!

A purple one, it's surely sly,
With whispers of how to soar high.
While green, the prankster, rolls in glee,
Just watch it tie itself to a tree!

Dance with colors, skip with glee,
In this wacky band of me.
Who knew that simply wearing flair,
Could turn the day into a dare?

Weaving Waves

Threads that twist and twirl around,
Creating vibrations, loopy sound.
With every flick, they start to sing,
Like rubber bands inside a sling!

Each hue a giggle, each stretch a cheer,
Bringing laughter, far and near.
A dance of colors, oh so bright,
Turning dull days into pure delight!

They wave as I run, back and forth,
These joystrings giggle, for what it's worth.
Splashing laughter with every move,
Giving all my blues a groove!

Oh, the mischief they conspire,
Ties so silly, they never tire.
A swirling party on my wrist,
In this colorful chaotic bliss!

Ties of Truth

Little loops of vibrant hue,
Connected stories, old and new.
Each twist holds laughter, deep in seams,
Where whimsy dances, and no one sleeps!

These quirks and quirks, they shan't untie,
Carrying the tales I can't deny.
The pinky promise, oh so grand,
Bound with colors – an endless band!

A tug, a pull, then off they go,
Chasing sunsets, putting on a show.
With every knot, a memory spins,
In this circus of wacky wins!

So here's to stories we all weave,
With ties of laughter that never leave.
A punchline here, a tickle there,
In these creations, joy is rare!

Spectrum of Stories

Bright colors swarm around my wrist,
Each one holds a funny twist.
They tell of laughter, pranks, and fun,
In the great adventure, we have begun!

One day a blue, it plotted sly,
To send a sneeze out to the sky.
A rainbow bursts at cheerful chance,
As bracelets join in a silly dance!

These playful ties weave tales unique,
With colors bold, they start to speak.
As smiles flicker, giggles ignite,
A jester's feast, from day to night!

So here we are, a radiant gang,
With silly stories and laughter's clang.
Onward we march, the colors blend,
In this chaotic, joyful trend!

Weaves of Wonder

In a jumble of threads, bright and bold,
Fingers dance, stories waiting to be told.
An octopus on my wrist, what a sight!
It waves to everyone, day and night.

Colors clash and mingle, oh what a show,
Like a party of socks in a tumble dryer's glow.
With every twist, a laugh spills free,
Fashion's a circus, come join the spree!

Twinkling knickknacks, a dazzling display,
Adventuring with style, come what may.
Catch me in pastels or neon so bright,
Making friends with a smile, that's the delight!

A collection of giggles wrapped up in string,
Each little charm a goofy wink, a fling.
So gather your trinkets and watch them prance,
In these playful weaves, let's laugh and dance!

Luminous Connections

Light up your wrist like the night sky's range,
Frogs and stars, oh what a strange change!
With glitter and glow, they jive and sway,
Each little bauble has something to say.

Riding waves of laughter over hills of delight,
Little flickering friends, dancing out of sight.
A magical spark, just take a glance,
You'll find your inner kid, ready to prance!

Glow sticks in hand, an impromptu rave,
As we rock a party from cradle to grave.
It's a friendship festival that never will end,
Shimmering treasures, let's twirl and bend!

Your arm's a canvas; paint it with glee,
In a nightly parade, come join the spree!
Connecting souls in a swirl of fun,
Together we shine, like the moon and the sun.

Cycles of Color

Round and round, what a colorful game,
A joyful riot, not one is the same.
From candyfloss pink to deep ocean blue,
Let's celebrate shades, oh what fun to pursue!

In circles we twirl, a merry-go-round,
With laughter and brightness, joy is profound.
Like rainbows that dance, they gleam and smile,
Hop on this carousel, let's go that extra mile!

Each twist and turn, an unexpected hue,
It's a technicolor world, just me and you.
Spin, then twist, as the colors bloom,
In our carnival of dreams, there's always room!

With spectral delights, let's burst into song,
Where hues meet giggles, we can't go wrong.
Join the cycle, let it unfurl,
In this vivid parade, we'll conquer the world!

Emblems of Expression

A badge of laughs with each funky charm,
Ticklish buddies keep my wrist warm.
A pineapple smile, a burrito so bright,
Who knew wearing food could bring such delight?

With every little piece, a story unfolds,
Of taco dreams and treasures so bold.
Each jingling object has laughter galore,
Wear them with pride, let's share the encore!

An emoji party, a mysterious quest,
They hold my giggles, simply the best.
From a winking cat to a dance-off prize,
They wink and they giggle, oh what a surprise!

Emblems of colors, from silly to wise,
Each one a portal to laughter's sweet highs.
So clasp those treasures, and let's be free,
Together in joy, just you wait and see!

Patterns of Connection

In a world of threads and hues,
We gather colors, make our muse.
Each twist and turn a story told,
In laughter's echo, friendships mold.

With bits of string and silly knots,
We craft our dreams in tangled spots.
Through loops and swirls, we share our fate,
A humor-filled dance, never too late.

Bright bands unite our joyful hearts,
In silly games, we play our parts.
With every tug and pull we find,
The threads of laughter, intertwined.

So come join in this colorful race,
With goofy grins upon each face.
We'll spin the yarns of joy and cheer,
Together crafting memories dear.

Looms of Life

In looms of laughter, tales are spun,
With every stitch, we have such fun.
We weave our quirks in every thread,
A tapestry, where smiles are spread.

With brightly colored strands in hand,
We tie our hopes, on this plane we stand.
Each loop a giggle, each knot a cheer,
In the grand design, we hold so dear.

Our crafts may twist and sometimes fray,
But laughter's glue will save the day.
We'll fashion joy from bits of scrap,
And wear our happiness like a cap.

So let's create with giddy hearts,
A masterpiece where fun imparts.
With every weave, our spirits soar,
In looms of life, forevermore.

Echoing Emotions

From laughter's depths, our echoes rise,
With every joke, we touch the skies.
In tickles and winks, our spirits blend,
A chorus of glee that will never end.

As moments bounce like rubber balls,
We dance in rhythm, hear the calls.
With silly puns, we strike a chord,
A melody that can't be ignored.

Our hearts are like a playful song,
In silly verses, we all belong.
With every chuckle, we share the light,
In echoes of joy, we unite.

So let the laughter intertwine,
In this grand symphony, we'll shine.
Together we'll find what makes us smile,
Echoing emotions, mile after mile.

The Fabric of Existence

In a quilt of quirks, we find our place,
Stitched with humor, life’s a race.
Each square a memory, bright and bold,
In laughter's warmth, our stories unfold.

With fabric scraps and mismatched thread,
We tailor joy, where none is dead.
Each patch a tale, a funny twist,
In our shared finding, none can resist.

So come and join this wacky seam,
In this crazy world, we live our dream.
With silly knocks and playful jests,
We weave our lives, and that’s the best.

A tapestry, vibrant and light,
In the fabric of existence, we unite.
Through every laugh, a heartbeat’s song,
Woven together, where we belong.

The Weave of Life's Symphony

In a world where laughter sings,
Threads of color bring bright flings,
Funky patterns twist and spin,
Creating joy from deep within.

A twist of fate makes us all dance,
In silly steps, we take our chance,
With each tie, a goofy grin,
A tapestry where fun begins.

Pecking hens and froggy leaps,
Giggling too, when friendship keeps,
Connecting dots, we surely blend,
As life's odd melodies ascend.

As fabric sways, the hearts collide,
With playful beats, we run and glide,
So grab a thread, let laughter flow,
In this wild weave, we steal the show.

Embrace of Echoing Tones

Bouncing sounds in merry glee,
A note slides by, just wait and see,
With wobbly beats, the fun unfurls,
In joyful jams, our friendship whirls.

Crackling laughs like soda fizz,
Riding waves of quirky whiz,
Each beat echoes a silly tale,
In the chorus, we shall prevail.

Tickled pink by rhymes we find,
A cacophony, lovingly intertwined,
With giggles soaring through the air,
It's a jam session, a lively affair.

From swirl to swirl, our voices play,
In schmooze and sway, we shout hooray,
A symphony of jest and cheer,
With silly tunes that bring us near.

Patterns of Togetherness

In a quilt of laughter, we reside,
Silly patches side by side,
Each piece a story, bright and bold,
Tales of shenanigans to be told.

Twinkling eyes like stars at night,
Forming shapes in pure delight,
With silly strings all intertwined,
In this dance, we are aligned.

A sprightly hop, a bounce, a jig,
Together we spin like a quirky twig,
With colors clashing, all in tune,
A lovely mess beneath the moon.

So come along, let’s weave this thread,
In the fabric of fun, where laughter’s spread,
In playful patterns, hearts combine,
As we stitch our joy, and brightly shine.

Tune In: The Art of Binding

In a world where giggles clash,
We weave our life with a vibrant splash,
With threads of joy, we snugly tie,
Creating bonds that reach the sky.

Tune in close, hear the silly vibe,
As laughter plays a wacky tribe,
With cheeky smiles, we twist and turn,
In quirky rhythms, our hearts will yearn.

Each knot a jingle, bright and free,
In this mad dance, we just agree,
To spin our tales in jester's art,
With joyful beats that mustn't part.

So grab a friend and join the ride,
In the music of life, come cast aside,
With stitches strong and echoes wide,
Together we flourish, full of pride.

Dynamic Threads

My friends and I are quite a sight,
With colors flashing, oh what a delight!
Each wrist a canvas, a story to tell,
As we dance around, weaving our spell.

The one in blue thinks he's a star,
But his dance moves? Quite bizarre!
In the spotlight, he twirls and spins,
While we're just here, laughing at his whims.

With every twist, our laughter grows,
The rhythm of friendship, everyone knows.
From silly grins to jumpy hops,
We bounce along, never want it to stop.

So here's to us, the vibrant crew,
With wrist decorations, oh so true!
We wear them proud, we wear them bold,
In our quirky world, our tales unfold.

Frequency of Feelings

In the air, a jolly jingle plays,
With every move, we catch the rays.
A pulse of laughter, a beat so bright,
Each wobble and wiggle ignites the night.

Our inner nerds come out to groove,
Bouncing to signals, we find our move.
With mismatched beats and silly tunes,
We march along, under the funny moons.

Moments shared, our smiles gleam,
Riding high on this vibrant beam.
Together we find a frequency fine,
In a hilarious dance, our hearts align.

So raise your hands, let's cut loose,
With giggles to share, there's no excuse!
In our little world, we'll broadcast joy,
Just friends and laughter—oh boy, oh boy!

Synchronized Strands

We lasso the breeze with colorful ties,
As we prance around, all laughs and sighs.
Steps a bit off, but who really cares?
Our rhythmic giggles float through the air!

Two left feet and we're still in sync,
Bright strands of joy, our own little wink.
Untangling knots with a smile and a cheer,
No need for perfection, just fun when we're near.

As we spin together, like leaves in a breeze,
Our memories twirl, aiming to please.
With shades of silly and bursts of delight,
We dance through the chaos, hearts feeling light.

So let's whip up a storm of laughter,
Crafting a tale that's full of rafter.
In this crazy dance, we're one big band,
With mismatched movements, we take a stand!

Interwoven Echoes

In a world of zany, we find our way,
With echoes of laughter, brightening the day.
Crafting our tales in vibrant hues,
In every giggle, we chase away blues.

With each step forward, we fall in sync,
Hilarity bubbles, a fizzy drink.
Like threads in a tapestry, we weave quite the show,
In this dance of ours, we're never too slow!

From silly stories to random pranks,
We deck ourselves out in vibrant ranks.
With flicks and flares, we bounce to the light,
Every moment treasured, a vivid delight.

So here’s to the echoes, the fun that we share,
In our jazzy chaos, we haven’t a care.
With laughter as glue, we’ll forever remember,
The bonds that we tie, in every wild ember!

www.ingramcontent.com/pod-product-compliance
Lightning Source LLC
Chambersburg PA
CBHW060112230426
43661CB00003B/166